D1240743

OTTER

BEN LADOUCEUR

Coach House Books, Toronto

copyright © Ben Ladouceur, 2015

first edition

Published with the generous assistance of the Canada Council for the Arts and the Ontario Arts Council. Coach House Books also acknowledges the support of the Government of Canada through the Canada Book Fund and the Government of Ontario through the Ontario Book Publishing Tax Credit.

LIBRARY AND ARCHIVES CANADA CATALOGUING IN PUBLICATION

Ladouceur, Ben, 1987-, author
        Otter / Ben Ladouceur.

Poems.
Issued in print and electronic formats.
ISBN 978-1-55245-310-0 (pbk.).

        I. Title.

PS8623.A 355770 2015   C811'.6   C 2014-908024-7

Otter is available as an ebook: ISBN 978 1 77056 417 6

Purchase of the print version of this book entitles you to a free digital copy. To claim your ebook of this title, please email sales@chbooks.com with proof of purchase or visit chbooks.com/digital. (Coach House Books reserves the right to terminate the free digital download offer at any time.)

I

THE
HONEYMAN
FESTIVAL

ARMADILLO

My lover spent his summer in the south,
carving armadillos from their husks. It was, to hear him
say it, an experience – the term people save

for the places they hate. He spent June in the sunroom
with a pitcher of sweet tea and a picture of me.
By August, just the tea, watching hicks

suck cigarettes through long, aristocratic
sticks, papaya seeds stuck between their burnt
sienna teeth. Everything was burnt there. My lover

carved years off his life with the very same knife
the armadillos learned to fear. *Where are they
now*, I asked him as snowfall took care

of the candles I'd lit. *The not-quite-rodents, not-quite-reptiles,
not-quite-right gatecrashers of the ark?
How does their nudity suit them? Do they sigh

all cool, how we sighed last year, when we threw our anoraks
off and found we had that chalet to ourselves?
If we were ever blameless, it was then. I held your locks

in a Chinese bun as you went south indeed,
throwing, upon my balls, your tongue, how sea urchins
throw their stomachs upon the coral reefs they eat.*

At which point my lover raised his knife
to my hairline, scalped me masterfully and poured,
into my open brain, a tea so cold and sweet.

Made of X's holding hands, squares
distinguished by squares, the west side
of the multiplex is an appreciation

of algebra. Annik
always hoped to make out
with a nameless stranger

as a box-office bomb blared
to an otherwise-empty
auditorium, as the score of violins

swept in to mute the audible
saliva. Now Annik is married.
She wrote me a letter

cinematic in its exposition:
*You faggot, I loved you. Of all the men
you could have been, you went only halfway.*

The measures and metres to which our lives
accord, the math that shows
on the sides of our buildings. Annik,

I still don't have the heart to tell you
we don't have any say. Our lives
are thrown over our bodies

like tides whose proximities
we underestimated.
I was halfway to loving

how you held yourself up
as if there were cameras
in all the rooms,

how your Eastern European comeliness
got so luminous, we
expected moths to round

the corners, carry you away
and drop you from such a height
the body would bounce upright.

OX

That was our last unripe year, rib cages bald, bright
and evermore palpable. The county's only queer bar
had just swapped its signage from hand-painted
to Helvetica. We drank as though new policies had
activated and we would not be grandfathered.

The men inside covered in slobber and glitter, I felt
unreflective, so filthy, a pauper. *Did someone
say poppers?*, Alexander would blurt, and his asshole
would begin to open wide. Outside, the rain arrived
as if under curfew. We had curfews too.

If I ever got a tattoo – I confessed, walking through
the dirty water, through the lightning's penmanship –
*across my ribs, a zebra mussel, inching imperceptibly
away. Something clever written in the slime of its meander.
Maybe 'epilogue.' Maybe 'occident.'*

Alexander protested, because everything I did
was on purpose. It filled my heart with helium. *Occident,*
I emphasized. *Not Accident. Ox.* His insufficient
moustache hairs caught small drops of rain.
Crickets scraped songs off their bodies with their legs.

HAPPY BIRTHDAY, THOMAS DEARNLEY-DAVISON

Happy birthday, Thomas Dearnley-Davison!
Sorry to arrive empty-handed. The plan
was to give you some tallboys, a carton

of Viceroys and a quality handjob, but I couldn't
find an unmarked paper bag in which to keep
the first two gifts, then to throw over your ugly

mug as I perform the third. Besides, it's time
to get to work! Just talk our ears off
about the nearest chip stand and you'll have

your writing den to yourself before the city owls
hit the hay. Then you can tend to a woman named
Marcie, a woman named Deb – and others too –

while they experiment with colour palettes, fondly
recall their ex-husbands and get to the bottoms
of their mothers' enigmatic dying

words. (Why do you write so much about women?
You aren't one of them. You don't even make
love to them.) Soon you'll be voting

conservative, snorting royalties off the back
of your own bestseller, telling some young
thing to make himself at home in the clutter

while you share with him your parliament of stories.
Until that morose night arrives, I hope you don't mind
if I keep calling you *Brother*, as if I never stood

in your doorway after a damp stroll back
from the moon district, wondering which beverage
you would nonchalantly offer me, ouzo or tea.

DERWENTWATER

Your taste must once have been
unwelcome, but now, like mucus
of the nose, it is a sugary testament

to ubiquity. How things do not change
but do dim.
In a dory, I paddled

into the lake called Derwentwater.
I was in its epicentre. I could go
no further in. Any movement on my part

would have been escape.
A lake is a body of water
plus the bodies of hundreds of birds.

I was a winged collective
eschewing you, a watery cavity, toward
a definition. The birds I was

forgot that names
are just ephemeral devices.
Your syllables – *er, wat, went, der* – had a taste

their gullets were welcoming to.
Nobody goes to that lake today.
The hostel beside it was sold.

We moved away, to dry, flat lands,
but I kept moving, all the way to Canada.
We wrote letters, until we didn't.

LIBRARY BOOK

Please write notes in pencil and erase before returning.
– Written on the first page of a library copy of
The Honeyman Festival by Marian Engel

Peter, dear friend, I write you from Ontario.
Often I feel that anywhere I go
there you shall have been. Certain boulders in the sea
follow whales obediently, such power
in the contrails of the beast. I hoped to be,

if anything, the whale, eroded, indifferent.
No matter. In the book, you marked with a star
every instance of a pregnant woman being
kicked from within. During a bath. During a bad
thought. To lift the reader out from a shift

in perspective. In worn red ink, your question:
How must that feel? I feel uneasy, Peter.
Inside me is a cavalry
whose conception, though so warm, wasn't
worth it. You are in Korea. The narrator's husband,

for sixty pages now, remains in Kathmandu.
Before you left, before you left more
sentences unfinished than you thought, you walked me
to the porch, told me which professors
to detest, which books to read, how love

toward women works. Opened your arms
like a bear finding balance with some difficulty.
I already know who shall die, who shall leave,
who shall learn what lessons. Still, I race
to the last page; soon, the book won't be mine.

CHOOSE YOUR OWN ADVENTURE

You pour your change
jar into his change jar and stare
into nothing for half of an hour.
House centipedes alarm you
with their conviction, their agility: they will go
where they please. You manage
to trap one in the hollow foot
of a candlestick.

If you spare his life, toss him
into the wild outside your window, thinking perhaps
he's got a small wife who'd have him
back, skip to the seventh stanza.

If you decide that he is an *it*, that its awful
and odd-numbered legs should dance in the water
you boiled, originally, for fiddleheads, procure
a Bible. Read, in one sitting, the Book of Isaiah.

❧

There aren't many faces
in your repertoire of faces. The green-eyed
grocer might be seen on Wednesdays,
his garbage cascading to dumpsters
below: potatoes with eyefuls of poisonous
growths, heartless artichokes.
Dawn after dawn, the body beside you
wheezes and brays and brings rotten
produce to mind, its nipples slowly softening
like radishes all autumn long.
That strange animalian
sound you can hear is the phone.

If you let it ring, fearing
your wife's baritone – husky and low
from a colicky infancy – begin
this poem again.

If you bring the receiver to your ear
and forget your son's age,
head to the nearest reservoir.
Remove your filthy clothes.

☙

You ought to yearn
more often – for a lucky
break, for a better mood, for an abode further
from the surface of the earth.
They're building Goliaths by the lakeside. The term
skyscraper has stuck.
You have been known
to pray before them. You're a conversation topic
in that neighbourhood – you bring garden
parties to life. The man who's got it all
wrong, whose knees bleed and not, some
say, entirely due to prayer.
Upon hearing your silhouette described,
perhaps your wife
has thrown a tantrum, or a flute of champagne
across a long room, then excused herself.
The afternoon you left her, she cried, *Go on and choose
your own adventure.* It's dawn now
and the man you love is in a mood.

If you think it best not to
touch him, then let his peril dissipate
into the ether upon which done things rest
and put this poem down.

If you cannot hold back, if you rush
under his torso as if it's an adequate awning, go out
back, dig a hole the size of a holy
book and await further instruction.

Alone clouds refused to cohere.
They darkened the city in blotches.
They rendered the city dalmatian.

I forgot my lover on the bus.
The brakes woke him up
at Abitibi and he found work there.

All year mosquitoes bit his fumbling frame.
The bites were like Grecian constellations
seen on a clear taupe day.

My Zippo was on his person.
I was planning to quit with the smoking
but how shall I now singe the frays

of my only warm coat? When winter arrives
the mosquitoes will expire
and material will cover the bodies of men.

At least I received a blank postcard
on the birthday of my lover, its message
white on white: *I am alive I am alone*

I am not willing to speak. Some men
are darkened, in the long run, by sun.
Others, more quickly, by clouds.

Hear me out, children of ink and strange ash. That lifestyle
is all about regret! Haven't you heard
how microchips are cleaned? With water so virgin, so free
of expletives, that it must spread the cleanliness. It craves

demise and detritus, would char the imperfections off
your rough, unleavened skin. I do spend time
being sorry, but who could forget the dark evenings
I somehow withstood, the long intact cocks in my mouth,

and I thought – *I am the water too dirty to harm him.*
And him. And him. Think of that
the next time you hold a mirror before a mirror
to form a funny tunnel infinity gallops through.

These days my sister taps on my front door,
wondering if I could babysit. I can even smoke her dope
if I light the incense too. That, my angry mob, is not
an offer a good man would refuse.

We've all mistaken laughter for permission,
but Illya, just give yourself a look.
Of all the half-employed, unshaven boys that could've
swung my howling body through the air just to exert
some power, who'd have thought it'd be the one

a woman has agreed to wed? This will end
how all the golden ages end – with a thud
and a bruised tailbone. Patiently, Stephanie
helps me off the ground. The two of you shared
a *pied-à-terre*, as young significant others,

wherein the inflatable mattress
slowly lost its breath to the weight
of guest after guest. One day,
there were none of those left. Their visas expired,
their internships paid off, their sweethearts

took them back. You suddenly had the place
to yourselves, and now, a new place;
some new selves. Illya, this violent little outburst
was probably just your attempt to make another
cardigan as filthy as your own. It's nothing

a half-decent drycleaner can't tend to, and you
can pay me back by bumming fewer cigarettes
until Stephanie dons the dress she'll only
feel the weight of once. All the most beautiful things
are things we rarely feel the weight of.

At one point within my lifetime
they stopped calling it *God's-eye view*
and started calling it *bird's-eye view*.
Below our Valhalla, souls of the mortal province

glimmer like sand in a furnace before
it is glass but after you could call it sand.
Valhalla, for now, is a set of guest towels, laid over
bitumen shingles. This isn't even my first time

being naked on a roof. That was in the suburbs.
I was an adolescent. My bright white accomplice
stomped on the gutters to make me fret
and weep for him. The kingbirds he teased

turned out to be countless. They gobbled
him up, into white snow. It was he
who informed me that glass-blowers die
if they inhale on the job. Air from the furnace

rushes through the blowpipe to scorch
and obliterate innards. He who convinced me
that even the husbands of glass-blowers
are right to sleep uneasily.

Next time doctor asks where
pain is, point to patch of dead
skin north of pubes, its receptors
lost in a chemical splash before
I learned to remember things.
Tell doctor *Everywhere but there.*
Screenplay idea: sad man jumps
off bridge, learns he can fly, flies
joyfully into jet engine. End
with a woman at the window seat,
slack-jawed. Dolly in, zoom out.
It is okay to spend money
on a good umbrella. Look up term
tharn. Ask Ryan what it means
to lose all your teeth in a dream.
Gut says, nothing good. The lover
is the default addressee. What's up
with that? Look into hypnosis.
Reply to Lucy. Mention how rabbits
run when terrified and freeze
when very terrified. Lucy likes
to know these things. What is
her brother's medical condition?
starts with J, maybe G. Involves
seizures, shivers. Shares cadence
with phrase *Be that as it may.*

Richie made me promise not to relate any stories of
embarrassment or crime, but, Richie, on
this, the evening of your nuptials, I must tell them about
our long day in Truro. I just must. The fallacy then
was a dark twin of tonight's fallacy, we
and the dogs – who are thought to be clairvoyant
on these matters – anticipated storms
that never came, and here we are now, beneath
a tarpaulin, on an evening they reported
would be clear and ideal for regattas.

As Truro woke, as Truro's rodents spat their
morning songs, Richie came across my notebook, open
to its core, and spotted my little admission:
I am in love with your brother.
The first line, I insisted, of a song I'd been arranging
to be played on the Wurlitzer, though now I
come clean, Richie, while your soul is at its smoothest
and most forgiving, I did love him, the crimson acne
flecked across his neck, he was like a man
a guillotine had made an attempt at.

We rolled that whole notebook into joints, didn't we,
Richie, then drove into the boonies to shove ammo
into rifles folk left above their porch doors.
That summer, your brother's motorboat
slipped into the Irish Sea, his mannequin body
demolished, and I'll bet he is here now, and is
glad, I am sure of this. Caroline, Richie
is one hell of a guy. You would do best to keep
his body firmly in yours, how seas contain boats,
for he is only stories to me now.

Text message from Daniel:

> *I don't know where you are but if you can see the point on the horizon where the sun is about to set, it's beautiful. The clouds look (1/2)*

And the second part never came.

That week the sky was always violet at dinnertime, and ducks always resided in its bottom right-hand corner, punctuation marks, to render the gorgeousness legible.

I left my windowless office and made for the waterside, the locks.

Violet and matte like a belly smeared in lube because the bottle cracked – how hard, that one night, did we laugh!

Something arrives and grants you faster access to those driest, smallest zones. Now I understand. I have been a problem. I have been ameliorated.

The clouds look what, Daniel?

> – *like the ghosts of men who died while procuring oil from the sea before you were born, before even I was born. (2/2)*
> – *like a type of candy floss they don't make anymore. (2/2)*
> – *so weary, from what, who could say. (2/2)*
> – *at me and I look at them and there is nowhere I cannot go, Ben, I have all the materials I need. (2/2)*

That night, Leah read a list poem of all
her innermost fixations and *how brave*, we
thought, *how novel, there is nothing left
to procure from her insides.* She skipped
the forty-seventh item, which was *oral sex.*

Later, at the Château Laurier, I wanted to ask the barman
for a pen, to write a little poem on a coaster.
I wanted to purchase a gimlet, drink
half then leave. I wanted to know what parts of the night
I'd keep and which I'd lose in my memory's

sly, ongoing cull. Or receive the wrong drink, flip
a table, tell the barman he'll be sorry –
Don't you know who I am?
The player piano wasn't played by a person,
but a person, long ago, encoded its cadence,

encoded its hesitance towards the coda.
As we speak now, Daniel, Leah's airplane
approaches a distant coast. To her left
are the Americas. To her right, a million isthmuses of ice.
She skipped the forty-seventh item because the parents

of her lover were present. What if that were me?
Would I do the same for you? What if I lit a cigarette
with a complimentary match, at a big desk, near
a mirror, and turned to your face, abstracted
by linens, and asked if you knew who I was?

I've found a way to let you stay, despite
this nation's clearly stated wishes to be
rid of you. Let's shred that deportation order

and make papier mâché centrepieces that are just
so *us*. We can honeymoon in Moose Jaw,
one stone's throw from the birthplace

of the chanteuse we both wish had never
caught, in her thirties, the jazz bug – but who
am I kidding? Neither of us can throw a stone

farther than a couple of metres. Which,
I was thinking, should be the distance
between our twin beds. In the mornings,

you can saunter to the sun district, window-shop
for must-have knick-knacks I'll later find behind
the sofa, bruised, broken, beaten. I'll stay home

handwashing the stains we don't discuss
out of your cape with the sequins. (Just joking,
dear husband. It's clear you'll never take

that eyesore off.) Perhaps we'll even
see each other, now and again:
from the neck up at the nude beach; from

the nipples down on smartphone screens;
or maybe just our eyes will meet, one cold
and cobalt evening, the rest of our faces

obscured by balaclavas as we happen
upon each other at the mouth of the river
we'll both have been hoping to skate away on.

HOSPICE

Small parasite you're
up to something
aren't you and aren't you
tired and aren't
you something. I took a trip

to the mausoleum.
I saw the velvet shelf Geraldine
will lie upon,
amongst amulets and talismans
and all the neighbouring urns.

I thought – what a magnificent thing
to be sad
in the spring. To greet
the neon green lawn with bare
feet and forget what disgusting

apocrypha lies
beneath. To make do with the
jurisprudence. To hold the jurisprudence
in small, clean palms
and wring from it a system.

II

RITES OF
SPRING

GULAG

Old friend, you've caught me
at my most lost, limp-limbed
in the gulag of unemployment.

I have become God's
ombudsman: he scrapes
his plate into my lap.

Remember that prayer I sent from
Verdun, as you shoved human
chunks down the mouths

of latrines, shouting
Worms, as ever, get the last of it! —
and I knew not if *it*

meant bone or narrative?
When I ask for that prayer
back, God changes the subject.

This is life after armistice, old friend:
leave to consult your advisor
and he'll leave to consult his advisor.

Give something
to God and he'll keep it
to have something on you.

FÊTE

I cannot stand a woman who offers nothing
to the world but aesthetics. She is aglow
this evening, arm linked with yours, lips

painted shut, motto loud
and clear: *Regard my body, gentlemen.*
Mark how it shines and suffices. The conversation

relates to, then resembles, war. Gentlemen,
can't we agree that few catastrophes
have sources as clear-cut as a bullet

in some archduke's jugular? The woman
removes you from the melee to the far end
of the billiards room: *Let's go home or to the*

jetty, she probably whispers, *where our bodies*
shall devise unpunctuated treaties. Your unceremonious
departure would bring to my mind

Passchendæle, if I had not slept
through most of those lectures. In fact, that course
was the F that caused me, on the morning

we met, to weep, as if my noble brother's life
were claimed in a boiling delta
and now I had to marry his hideous widow.

POLLEN

L'Hôtel in Paris, 1922: the gilded doors through which
a man named Oscar Wildebeest
exited, though his artistry and heart remained within.

Or was it Wild? Or were we? How I refused
to don the clothes the maiden ironed, but since
a promise is a promise, I sat nude while you drew

those ripples and contours, these fissures and nipples.
Then you threw the parchment and the pencils in the fire
which ate and ate like an armada of starved orphans.

The world without the window was just that, without:
what was missing singed our rote and smoky spleens
and there's a word for the crime Oscar Whatever

committed but I didn't care for those phonemes.
What did I care for? The tulips on the veranda.
The bumblebees that soared to the veranda

and took what they came for, shitting all over the elegiac
stamens. The word *veranda*. Mr. Whatever wrote a play
called *Salome*, about a sad woman. We laughed out loud

at his photograph: it was beyond us how so hideous a man
could bed gentry after svelte and nubile gentry. But he's got
a paradox named after him, and we don't even have names.

For shame, you said, raising a schooner of gimlet,
cigarette in hand. Years ago I quit but the carcinogenic
scent is now a ghost I find romantic. It gets my genitals

all hilarious. Despite the screen door's efforts to tessellate
your face, it was clear as the gin that we cleansed ourselves in:
your impossible handsomeness, mine to fail, to fathom.

I've just returned from a medley of Dvořák's oeuvre
as choreographed by Nijinsky and it was marvellous and you
and I are very different men. Would you agree? *Stop*. I cannot
imagine that one of us would donate his voice to the wild
to save the other from a transmogrification: to vagrant,

to swan. Let alone while singing in Czech. Diaghilev spent
wartime in assorted sanatoria, each closer to the north horse
latitude than the last. From a box seat he slobbered
over us, Slavic incantations mired in saliva – I'm just about
to wash my hair. The Tommies in their gas hoods

were one breed of ghost and Diaghilev, tonight, was quite
another. He was silver with no need for sheen, a careful way
of saying he was grey. Nijinsky once told him, *We must
cut it out now, Brother, I've got a wife in the works, it's
time we responded to our bodies – well fine, I'll say*

*instead that it's time I responded to mine, c'mon, Brother, any
face but that one.* From that confession onward
Diaghilev's hue would only dull. The ballerinas
once resented his inattention, then chalked it up to
providence. Brown, they reasoned, was the colour his dick

was meant to pursue, for providence said so. I need you
to answer me with silence. The messenger boy's empty
satchel shall suffice. Sorry for all the postscriptums
of gossip and rhetoric, but the ballet is a mask
that keeps me going. It has taken the piss cloth's place. *Stop.*

GLASS

The first time you answered
a telephone. *I don't like this*, you

shouted. *I feel as though your low
voice, without home, has come*

*to my face to beg tenancy, but I
already have one of those.*

We discovered
light is its own vehicle, it rides

on the backs of horses
made of light. In person

you took to saying nothing.
I took nothing to mean, *I am at*

capacity. I found your figure
novel, free

of curvature.
Then thought it best

to show myself out
the glass door –

the large, flat wall
light had no fear of. Through it

I could see a man
and, practically, his motives.

I spent my leave at Marylebone. The salad
arrived unassembled on a bald-cypress board:
whole apple, ham in sopping sheets,
rocket, acrid chutneys, burnt pumpernickel

crusts. Small wonder they bothered
to kill the pig. An Aussie
from a weaker sister infantry
took the seat across from me. Incarceration's legacy

perforated his vowels, made glottal
his stops. When he said *hysterics*
I heard *historics*. As in, *My damned battalion had me
in hysterics. Those fat fucks lost track*

of their duty – heard *Doty* – *always running
for the woods in pairs with women, they
assured me, on their minds* – heard *mounds.
Such useless base disgusting backwards*

fags – heard *fogs*. Fogs suddenly descended and it was
Ypres again, October, before I grew
my beard. I was assembled, digested by fog. Dew
between my back and fog's belly, fog's palm

in my mouth so I would not moan
audibly. *Clean as a bean*, fog fibbed upon
completion, and in the morning I would find
the leaves with which fog wiped away the fæces.

Calamities make entrances of exits.
If you do not
survive, you are remembered
as a change in weather: a fallacy, thrown together

pathetically – on which note the Aussie took off.
I clogged that establishment's toilet, then made
for the thoroughfare. Humidity was climbing
like a millipede out of an oil bowl.

*Would would it would it get would it get some would it get
some wind would it get some wind for would it get some wind
for the would it get some wind for the sailboat?*

— Christopher Knowles, 'Trial 1: All Men Are Equal'
from the opera *Einstein on the Beach* by Philip Glass

If I admit arithmetic
into the institution of my rhetoric
as ghosts arrive to empty my ashtray,
tune my guitar
and bring old friends to mind –

am I any closer?

If I decorate a headstone
with roses of paper and copper,
some crumpling in sun, some lasting
through all the future our instruments
can account for –

am I any closer
to the atoms?

If I assume it's beginning to rain
not because of wet polyrhythm on my roof,
not because of drops caught
in the lamplight that stretches through
my chest and halts at the first opaque bone,
but because, unexpectedly, I am sad –

am I any closer
to the atoms, to the details of the world?

Am I any closer
to the details my beloved
has become?

GODDAUGHTER

Forget slow
and steady – that fable's
only moral is: don't take

naps. Story time was followed
by a pantomime.
A servant suddenly said

what the audience was
thinking, so an empress
stabbed his bare chest

with a parasol. We got
the message:
this is not a world

in which interventions
occur. Children delight
in looking men straight

in the eye and saying,
out loud, dark things.
You are nothing to me,

said my goddaughter as applause
offered wings to a fairy.
I wanted only

to nap. While actors gathered
flowers, she picked
at the bread I had baked for her

until it was nothing but crusts
she would give
to the beautiful animals. *Up,*

she shouted toward distant
lawns, as long brown ears
emerged along the surfaces.

NUNCLE

Our century brims with abstractions, with
clashes: I want to know its taste.
So I chase chocolate with white wine, pair
tilapia with a most acidic merlot.
My evening has been ghastly. I just got

some dark post. A former comrade found his way
to the Seven Sisters, where the moon
huffs waves fro and fro and fro, its breath
cerulean, embossed by frost; where the moon
makes the chalk cliffs cerulean too.

Blind since Amiens, he was led
by a servant of the Red Cross
whose face, I'd wager, was something to touch.
My comrade gave a measly sermon, then
jumped. The little letter told me so. A sermon

fell with his flapping eyeless body
to the sea and still, I'd wager, adheres to the lip
that has lost blush. I'm sorry to tear
up like this. If my wife saw this despicable
spectacle, she'd punch me with her rings

on. Once, in Dvinsk, the suicide and I
found a house already deserted. Latvians
had shat on every surface before their
departure. He turned his bright face away from what
a kettle housed, locked eyes with me and spoke.

I have one son within my marriage, one without it.
How ghastly that half my pedigree shall occupy
our world, and half shall orbit. At once
we made for the nearest bed, and I'd wager
you know what we found there.

SOMDOMITE

Decay of this calibre
makes bastards of gentlemen, dandies
of warriors. Truth has become grounds
for a lawsuit, cries of slander scarce heard amid
tectonic shifts. Now the snakes St. Patrick missed

perform three-point turns to study
the skin they have shed. Long ago, one of our poets
received a little note: *My son has grown*
to adore you so I fear I have no son.
Best Regards Etc. For Oscar the Somdomite.

Audacity did not infuriate Oscar; misprints did.
He decided to sue the pants off this father of
nothing and lost and lost
everything. Now Ireland's finest, full of old
bullets, slip dicks into the low holes men are born with,

fearing the ammo they house
has turned them into weaponry. *What if that fatal*
mechanical blast is much like the blast that's so near
I can smell it from here? What if the exit
wound mars the white belly my palms

demand to cradle? A gas cloud is always about
to descend. A Black Irish Tommy shoves shale
in his pockets, purls them shut, scans
the ordnance survey for a corpse
of water deeper than he is tall.

APOLOGIA

The gulls hatch
plans and eggs
in the descenders
of this town's
nasty signage.
Brother, take
my rations, take
my word. Better
to be safe than
to be what I
spend my every
awake hour as.

Puberty and wartime
don't count: I don't
have many years to
my name. My name
is Siegfried. What
I remember is the white
of my mother's dinner
plate. *It isn't*
a diet, she said.
I'm simply never going
to eat again. I
asked father if we
ought to worry. *Look*
beneath the lilac tree
he retorted, *Look, it's*
Mildred, isn't she
pretty? None of this
counts. When Wilfred
died, I was sleeping
in an armchair.

The Celtic Cross Spread
has informed me I've
got one life left.
My name remains, his
becomes Roy. Magic
is our livelihood, our
gift to the coherent
world. One of our
white tigers reaches
to save him from
a tumble and tears
his head like a walnut
tree leaf. The tiger

is called Montecore.
Good breaches that mouth
of blood: Roy's first
words in our new
life – for everything
is new and red from
here on in – articulate.

Make sure no harm
comes to Montecore,
he somehow screams.
Montecore is a good cat.

BIJOU

I dreamt Wilfred lived, he and I
found a pair of boring sisters

who left us mostly to ourselves,
we wed them. I was a bolt of lightning the day

he exploded: the word for me failed
to designate the sound I later made –

the silence that followed that brightness
was an orifice so wide you'd fit

a fist in. Tonight I am a man, I am
awake, I watch moths battle glassware

and I sing interludes in a cant slang called
Polari, from a terribly odourless bed:

*Here with my little cove, warm and carts
to carts, our clobbers off,*

*we shall aunt nell to the alight
vogues, we shall lean closely*

*in. Both of us at our most alamo –
like puppies that no one neutered.*

No soap for the washcloth, no salt for the brine
that is dinner tonight. Mercury columns
insist the cold is too much for a man to endure

but, closer than ever to God, what you do
is endure and endure. With grit. Other inmates
use their washcloths wrong, weave sheepshanks

well into the black time, climb their new ropes
out of the dungeon, out of the range
of exquisite redemption, as the first birds

scream. Once it's the sun time, they toss rocks
they're tied to off a bridge – but which partition
hope their speeding chests to pierce?

All the ocean in this *soi-disant* world wouldn't
be enough for their baptism. Beneath
that surface dwells a door that's very locked.

Water would be nice, you suppose, but God
bleeds no fluid when you wound him.
His arteries, if pierced, fart dust.

Nevertheless, the smallest drop would do –
just one lick, from one stalactite! The ocean
and the heavy rain and the morning dew

and the rations your cleaved lips find ample
and the tears of other, better-behaved
men would be yours to yank tempests from.

PRINTOUT FOUND IN BOTTLE FOUND IN THE RIVER AARE

This of course is not.
My handwriting nor a product.
Of the Underwood typewriter you gave.
Me on my birthday I write you.
Via computer forgive my abrupt line.
Breaks this is a new.
Voice for me.

We don't write the world we.
Select epitaphs we poach.
The world's verbs and let them.
Do the writing us scientists.
Us mathematicians words.
Are simply game to us don't.
Be cross it has not collected.
Dust I speak of the Underwood.

Theorems are my water I turn.
Them into wine words.
Fail me now like they did.
When we rode your Vespa.
Through Bern which you pronounced.
Burn it was adorable words.
Normally fail me that's how.
Come we left the poetry.
To you the poetry and the driving.

From our bivouac we watched.
And were upended by the Swiss azure.
Beauty of the mountains you reached.
Out I said don't touch me.
At night touch me when day breaks.

You were a populous lodging.
For words you leaked them even.
In your sleep.
At the feet of Bern.
At the stroke of midnight you mumbled.
He is going to leave me but is he going.
To miss me this is the question.
That upends me.
I was awake I was being failed by something.
What few good words I have I have.
Stolen from you.

Remember there was no running.
Water at our campsite so as we drove.
Back to the hideous remainder.
Of the world you kept your index.
Finger in the air to avoid.
Smearing fæces on the handlebars this.
Is torture you said pure torture.

I was astonished by your way.
With words that sublime.
Drive was a perfect.
Example of torture and of purity I do.
Miss you most certainly.

Do you rage in space.
Do you ride a Vespa made.
Of bosons through the early.
Evening of the universe to find.
Unlikely words my little poet.
My little pilot answer me do you.

FOSSIL

Now men embroider tortoises
with opals and lime from the kiln.
At garden parties they discuss

Scheherazade as reptiles sparkle
near their feet, tumblers of viridian
booze on their shells, the creatures trudging

clique to clique. I hear
they never die. Their time slows down
and down to a limbless crawl.

November nights, I'd wonder
which stories, which faces
these everlasting animals might share

with the world our nephews
shall superintend.
Now I divide my thoughts evenly

between former lovers, former
homes and whatever imagery
has most recently disembowelled me.

BUTLER'S HYMNAL

I do apologize, my lord, but may I suggest
you pretend you're still tending heroically to the revolution
in Mexico, where they serve the red soup cold

on purpose? All sorts of bloodhounds run loose
and hump the collies – the offspring unsightly. I'm late
to bring the meal, my lord, because the tattoo took

longer than I'd thought. I scoured the Good Book
and got blood from that stone: God seems, at
worst, indifferent to ink, and rest assured, the waistcoat hides it

well. If you must know, my lord, it's a single word, perfectly
kerned, set in Bloodletter Grotesk.
No, it isn't the chambermaid's name – our schedules

haven't an hour of recess in common, and our hearts
not a scraping of blood. I share my bed with two footmen
while down the stairs, so many bedrooms desolate

as moons. Yes, my lord, a great deal did it hurt:
like my bones were being upholstered. What blood I lost!
I scooped it into phials and might, if it please you,

paint a portrait of her ladyship. After spotting
The Accolade by Leighton, I detest any artwork
that doesn't, to some degree, bleed. I'm just glad you

asked me to explain myself. When I last spoke out loud
the country farms radiated with paint, not fire, the city girls'
faces with blood, not paint. The world was not absurd.

III

DEAD DREAMS OF
MONOCHROME MEN

BARKENTINE

Black flakes fall from your stomach
onto my back: a small autumn.
That fresh tattoo, its scabs still departing.

A ship with three masts, all but the foremost
fore-and-aft rigged. The body above me
its overcast loch, speaking of the warmth

that goes away somehow. In this case,
with feet. To get the light switch.
Lube stains on your futon in the shapes

of hands bigger and smaller than my hands,
than yours. Toilet water outside the door,
forming archipelagos along the uneven cement.

Watch your step; leave me alone.
By which I mean, when you
leave me, please be unaccompanied.

EIDERDOWN

It's simple, even boring. All wounds are
good wounds, so long as you wake up
one morning – a man resting by your side, turned

away – and say to yourself: *All wounds
shall be good wounds.* One of us did this.
The other breathed, uneasily, his passages

dammed up with mucilage. Whose passages?
For that matter, down the back of whose leg ran
the blood, like a leash of foxes, darling

and crimson, while the other man folded
the duvet into eighths, the better to carry it
down to the bin? Conversation, later,

was also dammed up. Ergo it was
arid. Ergo nothing bloomed there, on the bald
bed. For every aperture, a coagulation.

MARIGOLD

As some scrotum
skims my tongue
like a dusted bulb
that might later do
an impressive bloom

I think of Paul
Monette in a bathtub
that's in a kitchen
asking his hosts
to scour his skin pink.

Paul later held his lover
Roger as he lost his
eyesight and enough
blood to give
a fruit bowl a fulcrum.

He is ambiguous here.
Some men can get away with
ambiguity. Tonight it is best
to forget whose bowels
are whose. Whose words.

I want to lose my legs
between our chests.
That is how little
room I want to ask
the world for. I'll be home

before dawn. *Home*
is the word that comes closest.
There's a door I will enter,
a grey bar of soap. A rosiness
I'll scrub my way to.

HOST

Someone leaves
the light on in the kitchen
and the shell of his egg

to bloat in the water
that boiled it. We go,
Oh, for this is not

a home. I love
and disappoint you.
If I pack the house key

by accident,
you're stuck in the room
there is no looking

out of. Dissatisfactions
brought to a murmur –
the humidifier, though

obnoxious, cannot allot
much cover. Know this:
the hunter does

become the hunted.
The singer, the sung about.
The occupant, a shelter.

Away to say the least –
even the mattress impression fluffed
out, even the bubbles

gone from the soda he chugged
most of, then left, for trains
are inflexible, they await

no man. I am a roommate:
if I am home, I say so
by closing the bedroom door

behind which we made a game
of keeping the sodomy quiet
all morning long. The first week

of a new lease is a tundra mnemonics
get lost in: once you're settled you forget
the painting of the caribou did not

always live above the white lamp.
You grazed every wall with its
back, unsure if it belonged.

The bedroom did not always brim
with such vacancy. First, someone
loved you while exiting it.

The sun gave our shoulder blades ulu-shaped burns, and the
sun gives nothing to our sort

I sleep now, and furiously

Clouds excreted shadows on the shoreline, and there were
no clouds

His body a train ride away, and nearby

There are organs I have never used before, and they are pale
from overuse

The sand had turned to pearls in our folds, and that kind of
sand does not turn to pearls

Then the carbon in our dirts to unthinkable diamonds, and
those were the wrong kinds of dirts

He occupied the wharf, and I occupied him, and I did not
occupy the wharf

Come adhered to bellies like white wounds, and sloughed off
like stormwater

I spoke first, and I have not yet spoken

He is moving away from the beach now, and he is absolutely still

We shared a heat, and had no heat to share

I am made of water, and he is made of water, and without
effort we breathe

BROWN STUDY

Flycatchers kissing insects
off each other's faces. The intimacy

incidental, here
in the feral protectorate. I liked it

when you cried. It gave my mouth
a hot place to get wet against.

I'd feel your body's resin
on my fingers, hours after, like ink

from a squid I had battled. Now our bodies
form the kind of isobar the moon

finds iffy
and turns its rays away from.

I, like most, have also turned away.
The firmament of days ahead,

telling me nothing
it hasn't told me before.

To shut the door, for instance.
And to have a seat.

TRIPTYCH

Subdermal cyst. Back of neck. Benign. Removed. His.

Sebaceous cyst. Right side of penis. Benign. Intact. Mine.

Varicocele. Left testicle. Benign. Intact. Mine.

All the most obvious route does
is suffice. By the time
we complete the Philosopher's Walk
there is more autumn
than before, and not one sacred datum left

to the imagination. If I change
into long johns, you need not even look
away. Tell me again
your dissertation topic.
Simony? I like that. The first man I loved

was named Simon, and every lover
since has been
a little simony. The olive Judaism
of Simon's skin brought pools of oil reaching
for the evening sky to mind.

His body, like yours, would lie
mute as a plum
until a vigilant limb came
to a decision. As you might have guessed
I've come to one myself.

THE MASTURBATING FLOWERS

Ignore me – I am frail today.
If I tell you to stop
walking, keep walking. If I ask

for a piece of your nectarine,
or press your palm
against my chest, where the ribs sink

most, where your come, months
ago, would collect and grow cold,
keep walking. All around us,

library books used to wilt and expire,
and if we were outside,
the masturbating flowers

would bite their filthy lips.
Sitting in the narrow shadow
of an infantile willow,

with a paperback, and a highlighter
to mark the words
we wanted in our lives forever.

The penultimate embrace, abbreviated
by such factors as the arrival
of the streetcar and the heterosexual gaze.

The ultimate, unabbreviated: a decadence
of unclean teeth. I've since begun flossing.
There's blood sometimes so oral

has been taken off the table.
A raw gum is a head wound, like any
other, a door a blight loves the sight of.

It gets men all choleric, though.
In the yellow light, with their yellow feet,
they push my body away.

It used to be a bank, that café —
you can rent the vault out for an afternoon.
Hold a conference. If you close the steel

door all the way, do not panic. There
are limits to the oxygen, and that's no joke.
There is no breath that does not waste or want.

Even when you spelled the word *caffeine*
wrong on the chalkboard, I felt compelled
to get you home and sit on your colostomy scar.

Infirmities marked by investments: yours,
an electronic dictionary; mine, a pair
of assless briefs that came with a reminder

to wash after each use. When I get
around to judging you, I'll do it how a dog
would. With the throat and the gums.

EDICT

The kindest thing one man can say to another is
I haven't come that hard in years.
If his chest ebbs like a slough you've got
your back to, if above your heads the moon
yaps, in its faceless way, to have

a little say, all the better. Absolutes
don't breach that place, and should be
so lucky: the great pull of a
rock in the sky dictates the motion of every
pint of sea and every pair of men

save, momentarily, one. The gift
your companion has crafted maintains an inertia
that's new to this world, and throughout
the denouement of lesser kindnesses your life
becomes, no others trip the light fantastic.

Moonlight is sunlight the moon intercepts.
In the years that follow, you rest your head
on pillows, chests and sandbanks, and every
shadow you make when it is night
is a dwelling seven words live humbly in.

I found myself speaking in doubles that evening.
Blame it on the chill, the advance
of the starrier hour.

Eye teeth seized. Across the heated patio
lay a squirrel's remains, perforated,
bothersome as all decay. He and I

both saw it. Neither man cared
to discuss it. The odd Band-Aid
along his crossed arms: several gimlets later,

I learned that everything else was shaved as well,
the chest like velvet, honeyed with the seam,
abrasive against it, and his, not

mine, were the shaking hands, then, as leaves
covered up the perishing jetsam
of the red season. His were the hands that shook.

REGARDING THE TWENTY-ONE-YEAR-OLD WHO
DESIGNS ROOMS FOR IKEA BUT INSISTS IT ISN'T A
VERY CREATIVE JOB, AND REMINDS ME OF THE WEEK
BEFORE A LEASE BEGINS, THE INNOCENCE WITH
WHICH WE SURVEYED THE BATHMATS, THE MANY
LINENS, THE MANY TYPES OF PILLOWS WE DIDN'T
KNOW EXISTED, AND I WISH SOMEONE HAD TOLD
ME THAT EVEN THE MOST PRECIOUS THINGS ARE
NOT IMMUNE TO THE TIDAL INGRESS OF UBIQUITY

Look at us, briefly
or for a long time, we share a need for haircuts
and a way with terminology. If there is nobody

who understands then I am willing
to be the one who understands.
If you require only parts then my home is a boutique

and I a dildo, a salt lick, a hole in the wall
as high as your waist. It
matters, but if only it had mattered.

TRANSACTION

His hairless Aryan body elongates its grace
into the room's dust, backlit
by television news.

Walls obscure stars. His hairless body is not obscured.
There is one source of light. It is not morning yet.
The television is muted and playing the news.

The sour white morning light
is on its way. If we could see the stars
we could watch them wilt. The length of his body
in terms of space. The length of its grace
in terms of time.

The back of his body is long and white
and acneous and not the source of any light.
The dust does not depart, or else it does, then more dust
comes. Dust being old skin. Stars being old light.
The front of his body is blue with news.

Every morning, a light that is newer than ever
is greeted by our oldest bodies yet.
His body, which elongates, used to be smaller.
Now it is bigger, more weathered, and the world
contains more dust.

Behind skin blood manoeuvres. Behind grace
lacunæ in the shapes of grace.
Behind the dust more dust. Behind the walls stars
then more stars. We are moving very fast.
We are staying very still. We are on a planet.

The moment that infinity diminishes, though
it did exist, I remember thinking, this exists. What it is
is inside one man. Then it is outside
both men. Then it is inside one man.

RUBRIC

Music and white share a source

Animals wince at the door

Armpits reminiscent of inedible flora

Within the mist a chest whose moles end sentences

Cleft lip

Testicular cyst

I could not love a man who was complete

Uvulas mute like those of bound bells

There is no cancer here but lesions like mouths

We will starve

We will have only bones to hold

What strange grammar the night has been known to bring with

A manoeuvre through glass

I love you less than ever before

For there is less of me

590 LISGAR ST.

I remember little aside from what was eaten, what
could pierce. At the supermarket, lobster pincers
were tied with twine: sad-eyed animals

to suck dry. At the apartment, one floor above us,
furniture toppled, Vietnamese children spoke
audibly and house centipedes ran for their lives.

I remember that love would be made, but later
and silently. I remember that photograph
everyone liked, with the ice cream vendor

out of frame, in which I look like a thug, Ryan
looks like a model and you look like a
child. Remember heat from the tree whose heat

was from the green season. Remember being shaken
awake, asked about *the bright intruder*. You'd been
dreaming. No apology because sleep is different.

There was nudity but whose? And whose
come, that one night, formed the shape of which
sea creature? On whose stomach?

When you finally came to rest, did the altitude
of my side increase? Did you fall asleep with your
body across my lungs? Could I breathe?

INTRAMURALS

Hands, unfurling hands, and bald
armpits, and hairy ones, and body
odour, and tank tops that had not

yet been grown into, draped
loose to reveal the acne defacing a
shoulder, defacing a back, or acne

scars, white hot, and tank tops
that were tight, and moustache
hairs, dark and sparse, like aphid

legs poking through bed sheets.
We watched from the bleachers –
the middle school students,

back at it for autumn, come
wind, come rain, and if
the boniest boy vomited into his

cupped hands, or cried out
for his stepmother, of course
I was going to stay. The brackish

filament the sky churned out made
promises it couldn't keep, of rain to
sluice off their reddening blemishes.

The sun did not arrive, later,
to cauterize the wounds,
nor did the twilight to cloak them.

BYZANTIUM

Say nothing here, but if you must
say something, say anything
but your rank, for a man

is a ghost with its shell
on, and it's not exactly
toasty in the alcove;

the boy with the mullet
would pull his pants back
up, if greater tasks

were not at hand,
like keeping the second boy
up in the air. A third on the

podium, a fourth behind
the blinds – he's of a generation
that forms sentences like:

Boy, did I feel silly after that mix-up.
Boy, do I know how to lay the charm on.
Boy, am I at a loss.

And whichever boy he is
referring to, the one with
all the answers, says nothing.

Dander from the alley cat that comes in
    through the window,
bloodstains from the bedbugs this skin
    feeds to brim – so worry
not, and scan the room for anything but
    exits, and scan these limbs,

and chomp their wounds – no, *harder* –
    like you've never
eaten food that was warm before. How
    swiftly your corduroys
fall to the ground; perhaps you really haven't.
    The bugs come with

the dawn, gnaw constellations into
    the lord I like to think
they take me for, never lower than
    the waistline, and that sound,
I believe, is the cat's tag, trembling.
    For all we know, he has a name,

a home, but wind and indigence have
    turned the text to meaningless
insignia. Now close your eyes, how creatures
    close their claws. Enjoy
immortal dreams of Technicolor men
    and I will too. I'll see you

in the monochrome their bleeding hearts,
    as red as Coca-Cola cans,
defy: no rib or skin to hide behind.
    Banish with the left hand,
cherish with the right. Flourish in the bedroom,
    perish in the light.

TOUGH LUCK

Friend of my lost and shivering youth,
friend with a lisp, and a missing dogtooth,
and a typo in his only tattoo. Did I

see you at the Yorkdale Mall, chiselling
currants out of your scone? I wouldn't normally
go there, I swear, and neither would you,

I am sure, but the shopboys down on Queen St.
gave my unravelling knitwear one stiff look
then shunted me up north. Good thing

I didn't join you on the indoor patio:
the more I'd whine about my trouble
finding wool tights small enough for these

lithe thighs, the more currants you'd discard,
and the harder you'd bite your fuzzy, white
tongue. We used to be young; we used to be

brothers. If it was twink night at Byzantium,
you would add me to your mailing list.
The trusty subject line – *It's Not Like*

We'll Get Any Sleep Either Way, Ladies! – is all
that kept me from shaking you awake
when we shared the southbound subway

back from Yorkdale. I'd never seen
a body get so docile. After falling nine
storeys a few weeks later, your body, I'd

wager, was more docile yet. The head
threw its blood south, a futile migration:
it clotted in the snowbanks, all primrose

and sickly. I was back on Queen St., so snug
in my new tights, and we will likely
never know if you were sad or stoned or both.

CADENZA

Was I happy with my diet that October?
Was I happy? When the elevator I was
ascending stopped and began to descend did I
weep? Yolky clots of cocaine dripping down
my throat. Did you read my tattoo out loud?

At the beach, or through a pair of mirrors?
Did I eat no fewer than two pounds of ground
beef every week? No more than seven eggs?
How did I sound on the radio? Were the eyes
of the white face you thereby envisioned

closed tight, all wet? You offered to first use your
fingers, compared the penetralia
to which cozy place from your time as a child?
Did God, in that sense, reassemble? How did
cohesion suit him? Did I genuflect and speak

with particular eloquence on the off-chance
those words were my last? Saying, *I am a forest
fire.* Saying, *I am an island and those as
we know do not cry.* Saying, *There my sea
legs are good gravy I have found them.*

That year I kept shortening idioms
to save time I did nothing with.
Life gives you lemons. Or, don't count your

chickens. I thought Michael stepped
on my foot, but no, that man was too
morose, his nose Scandinavian

and possibly doctored. Interchangeable men
pervaded in that pulpit. Look a gift horse.
Alongside other, slighter bodies, I did not

move, as if there stood a sculptress I, the most
poorly wrought Pygmalion, did not care
to woo. Instead I watched you dance

to the pop songs of joyrides and blindness.
Give a man a fish. Where is Michael now?
Were you not once his brother? Did you

not hold his shaking parts together
in the break room, insisting that he
was just tenderly vague in a world

that aches for precision? Pot calls
the kettle. That year, my wristwatch
was constantly broken. Always I fell

for its prank. We kept the world away from us
with barriers of sponge of latex of wool.
We wore earplugs at the venue.

We wore condoms as the day broke.
We wore toques whose pompoms
leapt off – *goodbye, cruel world!* –

because that year the cold came
quick. All of that is water now.
As in, beneath the bridge.

ACKNOWLEDGEMENTS

Thank you to my family, especially my parents Irene and Edgar Ladouceur. Thank you to Canterbury High School's Literary Arts program. Additional thanks to John Barton, Michelle Desbarats, Jeramy Dodds, Amanda Earl, Spencer Gordon, Collett Tracey and Jolene Wadman. Next-to-last thanks to the *In/Words* gang, with so much love and debt. Last thanks to Scott.

Some of these poems have been published in: *Arc Poetry Magazine, Best Canadian Poetry 2013, CV2, Dragnet, experiment-o, Hart House Review, The Malahat Review, North American Review, PRISM international, The Puritan, Ryga: a journal of provocations* and *The Walrus*. Other poems have been published in the chapbooks *Mutt* (Odourless Press, 2011) and *Impossibly Handsome* (Ferno House, 2013) and in the spoken word album *Oral* (The Moose & Pussy, 2012). 'Song of the Seventh Son of the Seventh Son' was published as a broadside by Odourless Press (2013). 'Gibraltar Point' is an occasional poem, written for the wedding of Stephanie Coffey and Illya Klymkiw (August 15, 2014).

Regarding headings: *The Honeyman Festival* is a novel by Marian Engel, first published by Anansi in 1970. *Rites of Spring* (subtitle: *The Great War and the Birth of the Modern Age*) is a book by Modris Eksteins, first published by Mariner Press in 1989. *Dead Dreams Of Monochrome Men* is a dance piece conceived and directed by Lloyd Newson, filmed by David Hinton, and distributed by DV8 Physical Theatre in 1990.

I gratefully acknowledge support from the Canada Council for the Arts, Ontario Arts Council, Council for the Arts in Ottawa and the Toronto Arts Council.

Ben Ladouceur is originally from Ottawa, and is now based in Toronto. His work has been featured in magazines including *Arc Poetry Magazine*, *The Malahat Review*, *North American Review* and the *Walrus*, and anthologized in *The Best Canadian Poetry in English*. He was awarded the Earle Birney Poetry Prize in 2013.

Typeset in Amethyst.

Amethyst is an old-style type drawn by Jim Rimmer for his Pie Tree Press in New Westminster, B.C. Rimmer based the idea on a set of roman capitals he drew in 1994 under the title Maxwellian, which were not released for commercial use but rather as a private type for his press. The letterforms are a product of Rimmer's calligraphic touch, much in the same light as his Albertan family.

Printed at the old Coach House on bpNichol Lane in Toronto, Ontario, on Zephyr Antique Laid paper, which was manufactured, acid-free, in Saint-Jérôme, Quebec, from second-growth forests. This book was printed with vegetable-based ink on a 1965 Heidelberg KORD offset litho press. Its pages were folded on a Baumfolder, gathered by hand, bound on a Sulby Auto-Minabinda and trimmed on a Polar single-knife cutter.

Edited by Jeramy Dodds
Designed by Heidi Waechtler
Cover image: Detail from *Tower of Babel* by Zachari Logan, 2011.
 Blue pencil on mylar, 15 × 120 inches. Courtesy of the artist.
 From the collection of Allan Thomas Jr., Raleigh, NC.
Hand lettering by Kevin King
Author photo by Corrine Luxon

Coach House Books
80 bpNichol Lane
Toronto ON M5S 3J4
Canada

416 979 2217
800 367 6360

mail@chbooks.com
www.chbooks.com